My Best Book of

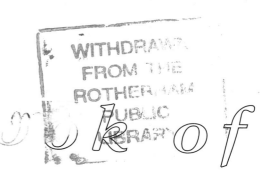

Knights
and Castles

Deborah Murrell

KINGFISHER

KINGFISHER

Kingfisher Publications Plc
New Penderel House
283–288 High Holborn
London WC1V 7HZ

www.kingfisherpub.com

Author: Deborah Murrell
Consultant: Professor Norman Housley
Editorial director: Melissa Fairley
Art director: Mike Davis
DTP co-ordinator: Susanne Olbrich
Senior production controller: Lindsey Scott
Artwork archivist: Wendy Allison
Proofreader: Sheila Clewley
Indexer: Rebecca Fairley

*Main illustrations by Chris Molan
and Mark Bergin*

First published by Kingfisher
Publications Plc 2005

10 9 8 7 6 5 4 3 2 1

1TR/0605/WKT/SOLGRA(SOLGRA)/128KMA/C

Copyright © Kingfisher
Publications Plc 2005

A CIP catalogue record for this book
is available from the British Library.

ISBN-13: 978 0 7534 1243 5
ISBN-10: 0 7534 1243 8

Printed in China

Contents

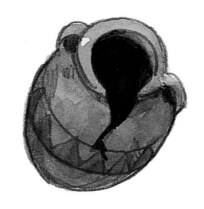

The Norman invasion

When King Edward of England died in 1066, Harold was crowned king. William of Normandy, in northern France, thought that he should be king and invaded England. He defeated Harold at the Battle of Hastings, and seized the throne. William, now called William the Conqueror, built many castles to subdue the English.

Castle building

The first castles were quite simple, and built of wood. They often consisted of an earth mound (a motte) next to a yard (a bailey). The height of the motte made it easy to spot enemies approaching, so often the owner built a watchtower on it. Soldiers could look out for danger through holes in the tower walls.

4

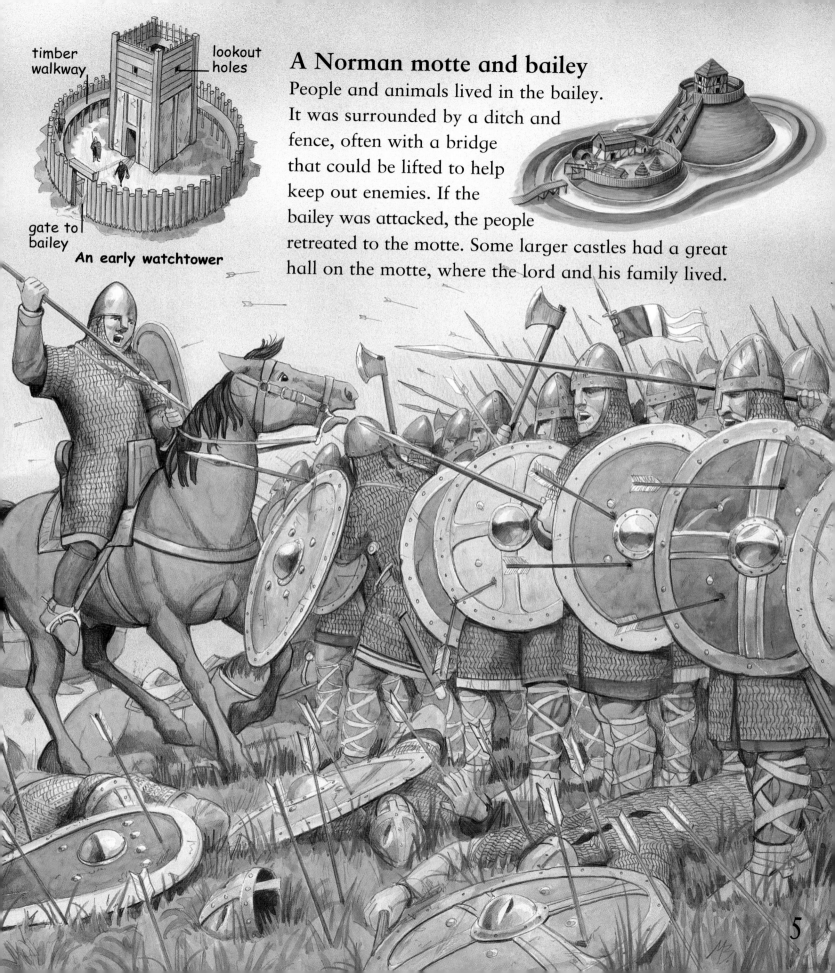

timber
walkway

lookout
holes

gate to
bailey

An early watchtower

A Norman motte and bailey

People and animals lived in the bailey.
It was surrounded by a ditch and
fence, often with a bridge
that could be lifted to help
keep out enemies. If the
bailey was attacked, the people
retreated to the motte. Some larger castles had a great
hall on the motte, where the lord and his family lived.

Stone castles

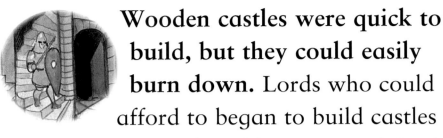

Wooden castles were quick to build, but they could easily burn down. Lords who could afford to began to build castles out of stone. A medieval king's or rich lord's castle would also have served as a garrison, home to the knights who protected him.

Master builders

Men who could design stone buildings were highly paid and well respected. One of the best known is Gundulf. He travelled to England from Normandy soon after William the Conqueror became king. Gundulf designed the cathedral and castle at Rochester, in England, where he was Bishop, and the White Tower at the Tower of London.

Fighting on the stairs

The spiral staircase was usually built with the central pillar on the left (if you were coming down the stairs). This meant that defending soldiers, who would be fighting down the stairs, had their right arm free to wield (swing) their sword. The attackers would be trying to climb the stairs, and their right arm would have less space.

Ivry-la-Bataille

This castle was built in Normandy, France, in the 10th or 11th century CE. It may have inspired castle builders in England to build similar tall stone towers.

lookout

watchtower

spiral
staircase

fireplace

arrow
loop

chapel

noble's
bedchamber

great hall

musicians

jester

toilets

armoury

cellar

well

prison cell

store room

7

Medieval life

Medieval kings divided their land among the nobles, who were also usually knights. In return, the nobles promised to fight for the king when needed, and to supply other knights for fighting. These knights often lived in the noble's manor house, and helped to protect it. Most of them came from quite wealthy families as training and arming a knight was an expensive business.

Describing a knight
The word for a knight was different in each country. In Spain they were called 'caballeros' and in France 'chevalier'. Both meant a warrior who fought on horseback.

Kneeling knight
Knights were expected to behave very politely and humbly to noblewomen. This knight is kneeling to receive a 'favour' (scarf) from the lady.

A knight might carry a favour at a tournament.

A reeve, or overseer, might be in charge of other peasants.

The king also gave land to the bishops and abbots. Many of them were as powerful as the nobles. Religious men and women were often the best educated people in society.

Men, women and children all worked in the fields at harvest time.

In return for farming the lord's land, peasants were allowed to farm a small area to feed themselves and their family.

Becoming a knight

There were three stages to becoming a knight. From about the age of seven, boys would be sent to the home of a lord. They were called pages, and they served the lord and lady, and learned basic social and fighting skills. From the age of 14, pages who had succeeded in the basic training became squires. They learned more advanced fighting skills and acted as a knight's assistant. A squire would hope to be knighted by the time he was 21 years old.

A page's lessons

Pages had to learn how to fight with swords and other weapons. For safety, they practised with weapons made of wood. Pages also had to learn Latin. They were usually taught by the chaplain.

Before being allowed to ride a real horse, a page had his first riding lesson on a wooden horse. This was safer and also avoided the risk of expensive horses being injured in training.

10

From squire to knight

Only the king or another knight could make a squire into a knight. He did this by tapping him on the shoulders and head with a sword. This was called 'dubbing'.

squire

11

Armour and weapons

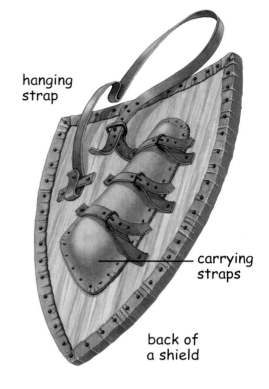

hanging strap

carrying straps

back of a shield

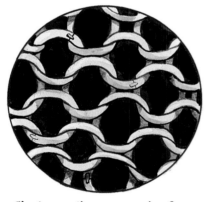

During the Middle Ages, there were many advances in the armour and weapons that knights used. Early armour was chain mail, which protected a knight against slashing blows. Later, plate armour became available. This was more protective, but also more expensive. Only very wealthy knights could afford horse armour.

Shields were made of wood. Early shields were almost as big as the knight. As time went on and armour became more effective, shields became smaller.

Chain mail was made from many interlocking rings.

Chain mail had to be cleaned of rust by rolling it in sand.

Extra padding

Chain mail was made of thousands of tiny iron rings. Knights wore a padded vest or shirt underneath, which helped protect them from heavy blows. It also helped stop the mail scratching their skin and making them uncomfortable.

Armour plating

Plate armour was made of metal sheets. The knight's knees, elbows and other joints were covered with many overlapping pieces. These were loosely joined together, so that he could move his arms and legs.

Chain mail and plate armour weighed about the same. Plate armour felt lighter to the person wearing it, as the weight rested more evenly on the body.

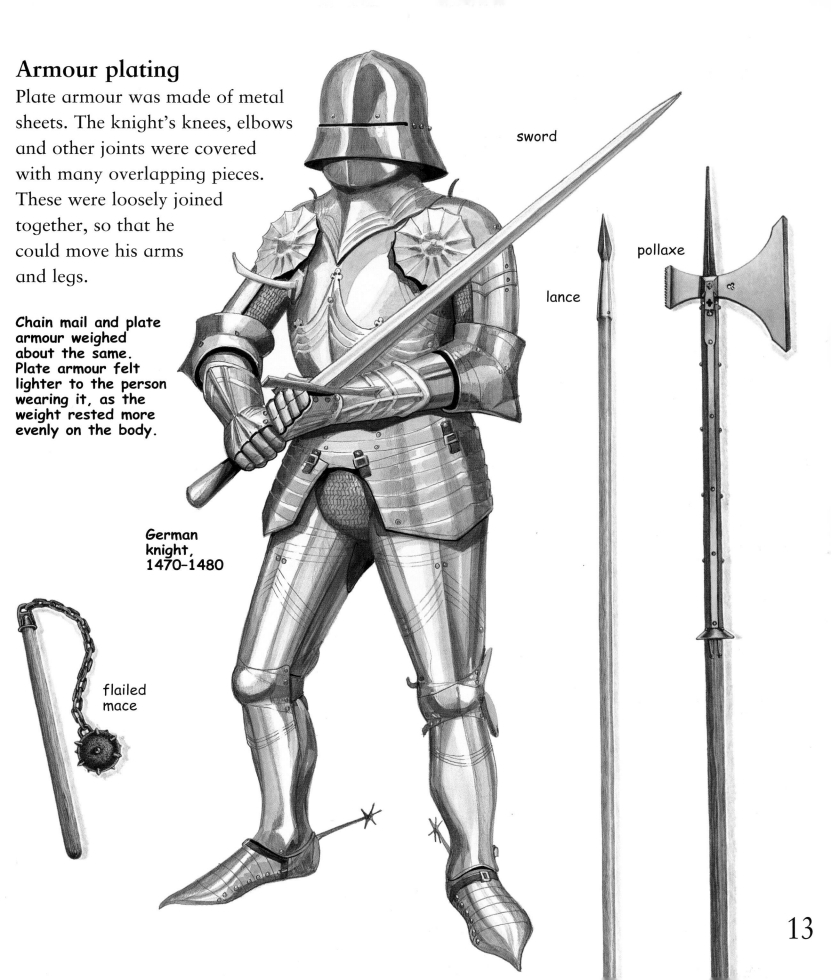

sword

lance

pollaxe

German knight, 1470–1480

flailed mace

13

Heraldry

When knights wore armour and helmets it was difficult to tell them apart. They began to wear symbols on their tunics, shields and helmets so that other knights could recognize them. These symbols developed into coats of arms. Families, towns and even business companies still have coats of arms today.

A city crest

This coat of arms belongs to the city of Lancaster, in England. The words read 'Luck to Loyne', which is the river from which the city took its name.

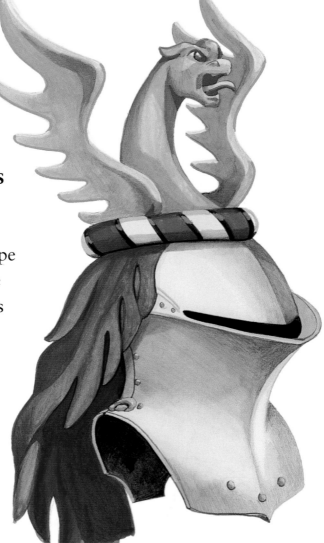

Helms and crests

In tournaments, knights often wore a great helm. This type of helmet covered the whole head, with slits to see through, and holes for breathing. A helm hid the face, so many knights added a crest so that people would know who they were.

Mythical creatures

Many crests and coats of arms showed mythical creatures. The unicorn is a symbol of purity and virtue.

14

Tree of chivalry

A real or artificial tree of chivalry was often used at a tournament. Heralds hung their knights' shields on the tree to show who was taking part in the competition.

Tournaments

When they were not at war, knights practised their skills by fighting each other in tournaments. There could be several events in a tournament, including jousting. Early jousts were violent and dangerous, so people invented rules to make them safer.

Jousting

In a joust, two knights rode towards each other, aiming their lances at the other's shield. They won points if they hit the shield, and lost them if they broke the tip of their lance on the other knight's lance.

swan crest on the helm

specially shaped shield to steady the lance

A knight who knocked another knight off his horse won maximum points.

Fighting before a battle

When they were away from home, knights got bored. They often organized tournaments between opposing armies. The heads of the armies tried to stop these events, as knights could die before the next battle.

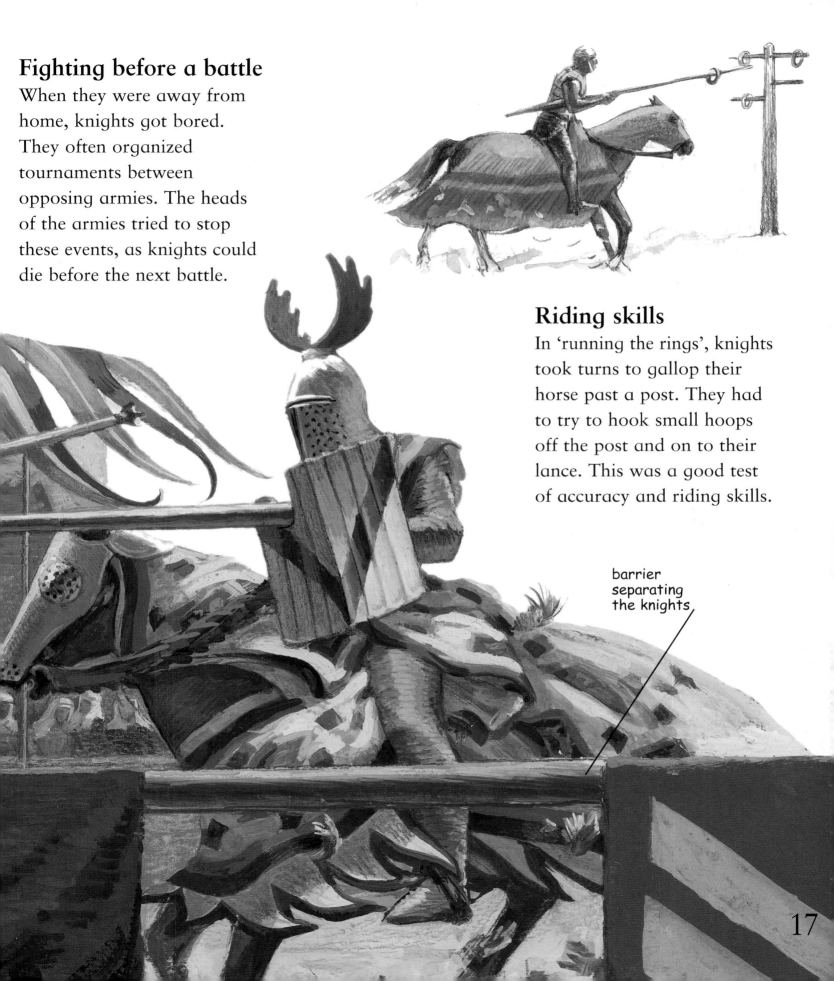

Riding skills

In 'running the rings', knights took turns to gallop their horse past a post. They had to try to hook small hoops off the post and on to their lance. This was a good test of accuracy and riding skills.

barrier separating the knights

17

Holy wars

Jerusalem, in Israel, was a holy place for Muslims, Christians and Jews. It was ruled by Muslim peoples, who allowed Christians to travel there safely. Then Muslim Seljuks took control, and it became dangerous for Christians to go to the Holy Land. The pope called for Christians to lead a crusade (a holy war) against the Seljuks. This began centuries of fighting in the Middle East and Europe.

Richard I

The king of England, Richard I (1157–1199), won great fame for his fighting against the Saracens – the name the Christians gave Saladin's army.

Saladin

In 1099, the Christians captured Jerusalem. The Christians ruled the Holy Land for almost 100 years. In 1187, Saladin, the ruler of Egypt, united the Muslims and recaptured it. Saladin was one of the most civilized rulers in the world at the time. When Richard I had a fever, Saladin sent him snow to cool him.

Both Saracens and Christian knights fought on horseback.

A Crusader castle

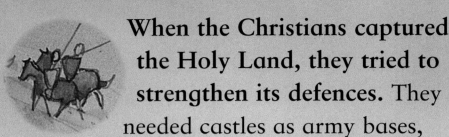

When the Christians captured the Holy Land, they tried to strengthen its defences. They needed castles as army bases, and to guard roads and borders. Krak des Chevaliers was a small Muslim fortress. The Christian Hospitaller knights rebuilt it, adding two solid outer walls.

lookout tower

commander's room

aqueduct

water reservoir

A winning trick

The Christian Hospitaller knights held Krak des Chevaliers from 1124 to 1271, when a group of Muslims called Baibars attacked it. The leader of the Baibars tricked the defending knights with a fake letter from their Grand Master, telling them to surrender.

main hall

inner courtyard

covered walkway

Fighting base
Krak des Chevaliers could house up to 2,000 knights, and could store enough food to feed a large army for a year. The castle survived at least 12 attacks before it fell to the Baibars.

Military orders

Some of the knights who stayed on in the Holy Land formed military orders. They lived religious lives, like monks, but were also highly respected warriors who fought for their religion. In the Third Crusade, Templar and Hospitaller knights marched at the front and back of Richard I's army, to protect the troops.

Protecting pilgrims

Knights Templar (below) promised to protect pilgrims (religious visitors to the Holy Land). Instead of the woollen robes that most monks wore, they were allowed to wear linen, because of the heat in the Middle East.

Going east

To begin with, Teutonic knights ran a hospital. They became more militant in the late 12th century CE, and travelled to eastern Europe to convert the Slav people to Christianity.

Healing and trading

Hospitaller knights looked after the sick. They owned a fleet of ships, which they used to trade goods, such as spices and silks, between the Middle East and Europe.

Siege warfare

Castles had such good defences that sometimes the only way to capture one was to besiege it, by surrounding it with troops. People built special machines, called siege engines, to attack a castle and persuade the soldiers defending it to surrender.

Slings and arrows

Some machines, such as the trebuchet and the ballista, slung stones and other objects over the walls. Siege towers carried troops right up to the castle, where they could fight the soldiers on top. Miners tried to dig underneath the walls.

trebuchet

Château Gaillard, in France,
under siege in 1204

siege
tower

miners

battering
ram

catapult

25

End of an era

By the late Middle Ages, the time of the warrior knight was drawing to a close. There were various reasons for this. Money, advances in weapons and warfare, and international politics all played a part in the disappearance of the medieval knight. Today, some countries still dub knights, but it is a mark of respect only, and knights are not expected to fight for their country.

Ruined castles

Many knights returned home to run their estates (lands). Castles were not strong enough to withstand cannons, so those who could afford it built stronger fortresses. Some castles remained, but many fell into ruins and their stones were used for new buildings.

Shooting power

Guns and gunpowder were invented in the 14th century CE, and by the 15th century they were in common use in wars. Even plate armour could not protect a knight or his horse from bullets. Many military leaders began to hire professional, full-time soldiers, who were always available for fighting and training, instead of relying on the knights to fight when they were needed.

Castles today

Some medieval castles still stand today. Many are open to visitors, and contain museum collections or other exhibitions. Over the centuries, people have added towers and rebuilt parts of castles. Some castles today look very different from the way they were originally designed.

The Tower of London

Since it was built, the Tower of London has been used at times as a prison, storehouse and museum. The White Tower, completed in about 1097, was the first stone keep in England. It is one of the most popular tourist attractions in Britain.

Beefeaters, the Tower's guards, give daily tours for visitors.

Saumur castle, France

The castle of Saumur was built in the 14th century CE. Today it is open to visitors, and contains a museum with a collection of medieval art.

How do we know?

We can find out about about **knights, castles and medieval life from many things.** Some castles and their contents, such as furniture and common household objects, have survived. These tell us what life in a castle was like. Stories and letters tell us what people found interesting. Even tombstones can tell us what kinds of clothing and armour people wore.

Hidden history

Sometimes, medieval floors lie underneath more recent ones. Archaeologists uncovering them take great care not to damage them.

30

Glossary

aqueduct A man-made channel created to move water from a river or lake to a town or building.

archer A soldier who fought with a bow and arrows.

armoury A place where arms, or weapons, were stored.

arrow loop A slit in the side of a castle or other building, used for firing arrows through.

battering ram A heavy object, often a wooden beam, which attackers swung or rammed against a door to break it down.

cannon A large, heavy gun, used in warfare to fire cannonballs.

catapult A machine used to throw large rocks or other heavy objects.

chaplain A religious man who worked outside of the church.

favour An object, such as a handkerchief, which a noble lady gave to a knight to wear to show his loyalty to her.

garrison A group of soldiers who defended a castle, fortress or town, and also the building or part of the building in which they lived.

great hall A castle's main area, where people ate, held meetings and slept.

jester A joker, paid by a noble family to entertain them.

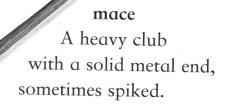

mace A heavy club with a solid metal end, sometimes spiked.

medieval Relates to the Middle Ages.

Middle Ages A period of history in Europe, often said to be from about CE1000 to 1500.

pollaxe A long weapon with a hammer or spiked axe on the end.

siege tower A tall tower with a stairway that could be wheeled up to a castle. Soldiers climbed up it to enter the castle over the walls.

trebuchet A type of catapult with a long, weighted arm, used to throw objects over castle walls.

Index